Life, Love
and all the other
Stuff

Nicky Wildman

authorHOUSE®

AuthorHouse™ UK Ltd.
500 Avebury Boulevard
Central Milton Keynes, MK9 2BE
www.authorhouse.co.uk
Phone: 08001974150

© *2008 Nicky Wildman. All rights reserved.*

No part of this book may be reproduced, stored in a retrieval system, or transmitted by any means without the written permission of the author.

First published by AuthorHouse 4/21/2008

ISBN: 978-1-4343-7519-3 (sc)

Printed in the United States of America
Bloomington, Indiana

This book is printed on acid-free paper.

DEDICATION

For Mum, and my sister Cindy for always being there and for my three sons Luke, Sam and William.

POEMS

DEDICATION	1
MUM	7
IF THINGS DON'T CHANGE THEY'LL STAY AS THEY ARE	9
I DON'T MIND	11
CHRISTMAS IS COMING	13
THINGS KIDS DO	15
LIFE	17
OUTSIDE PACKAGING	19
HAPPINESS	21
HOME TO THE LIGHT	23
WHO HAS THE RIGHT TO JUDGE	25
WHAT DOES GOD LOOK LIKE?	27
DOES IT MATTER	29
YOU'LL FIND ME THERE	31
A SMILE	33
PUT YOUR TRUST IN ME	35
ENJOY THE PRESENT MOMENT	37
DRIVING FORCE	39
MOVING ON UP	41
MORE THAN I CAN SAY	43
WHAT AM I?	45
MOVING ON	47
IT'S NOT FAIR	49
SORRY I'M LATE	51
RAINBOW OF LIFE	53

GRANDAD	55
NOT GOOD ENOUGH	57
IF YOU EVER LEAVE ME	59
ARE WE THERE YET?	61
MY SON	63
MONEY	65
SISTER	67
EMPTY PROMISES	69
LOVE ALWAYS	71
FOLLOWER OF FASHION	73
BARGAIN HUNT	75
FAITHFUL FRIEND	77
A DRUNK MAN'S WORDS	79
SPIRIT OF THE SEA	81
IF I WERE A CAR	83

This poem titled Mum was what inspired me to start writing poems. My mum passed away in 2001 aged 77 and I know that where she is now is where she is free from pain. She suffered health wise in the last few years of her life as she had a stroke. I watched a lady who was active and always running around helping everybody slowly deteriorate. However ill she must have felt, she never complained and still managed to keep her sense of humour.

Mum

Sometimes I feel you near me, as you brush across my head,
I cannot see your body but I feel your spirit instead,
When I have a problem I wish you could advise,
so I say the words aloud and you
seem to make me wise.
When you were upon this earth your words could be hard to hear,
but I know because
you've told me that it's because you hold me dear,
I realise now the reason why sometimes you were sharp,
you hadn't all life's answers
but now you hear the angel's harp,
I saw you locked inside yourself, you began to forget your words,
but now I know that
you're just fine, you spirit free like the birds,
You told me now you're happy and watching from above,
and when I feel you near
me all I feel is love.

I wrote 'If things don't change they'll stay as they are' when I reached the age when you realize the things your mother said were right. How annoying is that! My Dad also used to pass the remark as he had a rather dry sense of humour. He liked to test someone's reaction when he said it and see if they appreciated the obvious.

IF THINGS DON'T CHANGE THEY'LL STAY AS THEY ARE

I need to wear glasses the read the small print,
I can't read my map I keep having to squint,
I never thought the day would come when I'd be glad to wear my vest,
But I'm shivering like a puppy, so I'll be sensible like the rest,
I've had to buy flat shoes for work because I can't wear heels all day,
My Mum was right all along in what she used to say,
"You'll be sorry when you're older, you'll have to take more care",
She would wag her finger and give a disapproving stare,
Now I know just what they mean when they say everything goes South,
I said that wouldn't happen, trust me and my big mouth,
But although some things are changing, I'm still going to aim high,
Even though my bottoms sliding down the back of my thighs,
I'll just add 'support knickers' to my Christmas list,
But I'm not ready yet for afternoons playing whist,
Really I'm just kidding, I won't lose my sense of fun,
The person that I am is not ready to run,
It's not important what our packaging is like it's what is inside that's true,
So just be thankful with what you've got and be happy to be you.

I wrote 'I Don't Mind' because a few men seem to think that life is like a 1950's soap powder advert. The little woman in the sticking out dress, immaculate make-up, cooking the dinner. My life has never been like that. I'm usually trying to do something else at the same time as cook the dinner, so get a man who's partly house trained. My partner is quite a lot older than me so came already trained.

I DON'T MIND

I don't want to be the little woman dear,
I don't want to stand in the shade,
I don't mind washing your socks dear,
But that isn't my personal crusade.

I don't mind cooking your dinner,
I don't mind feeding the cat,
I don't mind supporting your projects,
But I don't want to do just that.

I don't mind wiping the kids noses dear,
And being at everyone's beck and call,
I don't mind helping when you've lost things dear,
I really don't mind at all.

I don't mind when you're untidy,
I'm not worried if you don't wipe your feet,
I don't mind if you don't buy me flowers,
Or that you don't put down the loo seat.

I know that you think that I'm dizzy,
Sometimes that may be true,
But don't think I'm just the little woman dear,
I'm a person just like you.

Christmas now seems to loom on us in September, I have seen Christmas goods displayed in the shops then. It is hard not to be drawn into the commercialism and overspend. Children get so taken in by the hard sell of all the adverts on the television but as long as they realize that they won't get absolutely everything they want then that's ok. The best part for me is seeing the smiles on their faces when they open their presents.

Christmas is Coming

Very soon Christmas will be here,
It's supposed to be full of good will and cheer,
But how many people are filled with dismay,
Too much money is spent all just for one day,
We buy too much food and expensive gifts,
We try to please everyone and heal family rifts,
There's no sense to it all, there's no rhyme or reason,
To act like this because it's the Christmas season,
Although it's good to give we get into debt,
And spend all year paying if off and yet,
We do exactly the same thing again next year,
Well I certainly won't of that there's no fear,
I won't turn into Scrooge and shout 'bah humbug'
But I won't be totally drawn into the commercialised club,
I'll still buy presents but not go over the top,
I'll still buy nice food but I'm definitely going to stop,
Yes, to stop and to think what its now all become,
A way to make money and its lost some of its fun,
So don't succumb to the pressure and please don't feel you're alone,
If you don't want to live up to the standards in 'Woman and Home'
Just enjoy time with your loved ones and rejoice and sing,
Be glad if you're healthy and enjoy everyday things,
Like a walk on a Winter's day when the sky's blue and clear,
Or to sit by the fire whilst your dog draws in near,
We don't need lots of money to enjoy a good time,
We just need each other and everything's fine.

'Things Kids Do' is a tongue in cheek look at how it is having children in the house. I sometimes wonder If my children think I've always been the age I am now, although the other day my youngest said I was like Peter Pan and I've never grown up. I'm not sure whether that's a compliment or criticism. Another of my sons when he was fourteen at the time summoned me for a heart to heart discussion. He looked rather sheepish as he told me I would be getting a letter from his school about being caught smoking. He had built himself up to me doing my nut, but as I already knew what he got up to I wasn't surprised. I don't think he understood my reaction. I told him I'd rather he didn't smoke but seeing that I couldn't be with him 24 hours a day stopping him he'd probably do it anyway. I told him I was his age once!

Things Kids Do

When your children cause you grief,
The things they do are beyond belief,
They answer you back and make you wish,
Perhaps I should have stuck with a gold fish,
They come home late and worry you sick,
They've always got an answer, they know every trick,
They raid the food cupboard and leave rings around the bath,
They think that you're stupid, you've just got to laugh,
You must be a never ending money supply,
They don't just WANT something, they NEED it, that's why,
Their bedroom's untidy, clothes don't go in the washing bin,
It's really no wonder the state that I'm in,
But really I don't mind because when all's said and done,
When I was a child I was a pain in the bum.

If we spend too much time pondering about what life is all about we forget to enjoy it when we can. With the pressure of television and magazines some people try to strive to an ideal that is presented to them that we need to look perfect, live in a house that looks a certain way, keep up with all the latest technology and earn lots of money to buy it. The more money we have, we seem to want more and end up with quantity but no quality of life. Everything is ok in moderation.

LIFE

Life should be fun, so have a blast,
Don't sit and dwell upon your past,
We just don't know how long we're here to stay,
So make the most of every day,
Sometimes things happen that make us sad,
But you'll win through so don't get mad,
Appreciate what you have and not what you haven't got,
Embrace life's changes and be content with your lot,
For life's a gift to be thankful for,
You'll never be happy if all you want is more.

The poem 'outside packaging' is about someone I knew who couldn't understand why life had given her a hard time. The way she treated people had quite a bit to do with it. People tried to help her, but one by one she drove them away and as far as I know she is still doing the rounds. Going from one person to another.

Outside Packaging

There was a young woman who lived in my street,

She had money, a nice house and everything sweet,

She was pretty to look at, she was slim, dark and blue eyed,

But she couldn't keep friends how ever much she tried,

Her life had been based on the outside façade,

She couldn't see further, she didn't need to try hard,

As she became older she did not become wise,

People tried to point out that it was not a surprise,

People grew tired of giving her the support,

Because really the ball was in her own court,

She relied on the material things in her life,

But they did not make her happy, they just caused her more strife,

What was on the inside she chose not to show,

She was vain and bitter, she just couldn't grow,

One by one friends deserted, fed up listening to her moan,

A sad old lady all on her own.

I wrote 'Happiness' because that's what everyone strives for and it's what it means to me. It took me a few years to grasp the concept fully!

Happiness

H is for HOLD onto your dream, for only you can make it happen,

A is for APPROACH, always try to have an optimistic approach to life,

P is for PLENTY of laughter,

P is for POSITIVE, always try and see it,

I is for INTERESTS; pursue them,

N is for NO NEGATIVITY, only allowable in very small doses,

E is for EVERYONE, I believe everyone can be happy if they choose to be,

S is for SPECIAL, for that's what you are, so believe it and other people will too,

S is for SUCCESS, Happiness comes from within you,

don't rely on other people to make you happy, you hold the key.

'Home to the Light' was written for a friend who took his own life in 1998. He kept how he felt after a series of life problems to himself until he could take no more. The last picture in my mind that I have of him is seeing him run across the road to his car late one night, laughing and waving. I had a conversation over the telephone the next morning but by that evening he was gone, having carefully planned everything and he left goodbye letters to his children.

Home to the Light

How could we imagine how you really felt inside,
You always seemed so happy but that was just your pride,
You couldn't voice your feelings, you couldn't bear the pain,
So nobody could help you, so no one is to blame,
For events just gradually snowballed and you masked the pain with pills,
But you really needed someone to give strength to your will,
You had people who loved you, but you kept them at arms length,
If only you had confided, they could have given you strength,
It was the light you craved for, to go back home to rest,
It probably was your time to go, you had not failed the test,
You'd probably gained the knowledge needed, for this time in your path,
You made many people happy because you loved to laugh,
You took the pills and drink to block out all the pain,
You left detailed letters leaving your material goods to gain,
Now you're safe and happy with spirit enfolding you,
You're with friends and loved ones and the pain is no longer true.

'Who has the right to judge' is about trying not to be judgemental. You never know what situation you may find yourself in and sometimes we don't know all the facts.

Who Has the Right to Judge

We can only judge by what we know and who are we to say what's right,
Society sets the standards and that's why people fight,
One disagrees with another when they don't share the same view,
It could be religion, politics, or money, just to name a few,
If we could only agree to differ and respect each other's ways,
Life would be so much easier and we'd all have happier days,
If only we understood this and took a different view,
No one should judge another, you wouldn't like it done to you,
We are all individuals with different outlooks on life,
But we weren't put on earth to be miserable and endure endless trouble and strife,
We are all here to help each other and be kind to our fellow man,
The sooner we get that the better, for it's part of the divine plan,
So try not to be judgemental and respect other people's ways,
Life would be so much easier and we'd all have happier days.

Why is it that people have to have a particular idea of what God looks like. I think it doesn't matter what our perception is as long as you have faith in something that's ok, even if it's just faith in yourself.

What Does God Look Like?

What does God look like?
Do you ever wonder
Is he short, tall, fat, thin?
Does he have dark hair or fair?
Are his eyes blue, green or brown?
Does he have a beard or moustache?
What clothing does he wear, if any?
Why do we need to know, does this make us feel closer by association,
and more able to relate to him.
I think God is a little bit of everyone, but something you don't need to see,
He doesn't have to be in any particular form,
He is the spirit that is in all of us,
That's why when we ask for help we are really helping ourselves,
So just remember to ask.

I always think it's good to have your own opinion but other people have a right to express their opinion too and it is not worth arguing about. If we could sometimes agree to differ the world would be a lot easier to live in so 'Does it matter' is about that.

Does it Matter

It's all too easy to criticize another persons ways,
Just don't sweat the small stuff if you want to live happier days,
What's needed to be done should get done, without harm to our fellow man,
Don't worry about technicalities, it's just not part of the plan,
Just learn that we're all different, who is to say what's normal or right,
If only we'd listen to spirit, we'd learn it's not worth the fight,
What works for me may not be right for you,
So follow your instinct and you will see it through,
You'll make mistakes and get, "I told you so",
But we have to follow our own path, for that's how we grow,
Listen to all the advice but make up your own mind,
Listen to the inner voice and your troubles will unwind.

'You'll find me there' is simply about never giving up on life.

You'll Find Me There

A mind in turmoil, deep despair,
You haven't answers and you don't care,
You've sunk into that bottomless pit,
No one can help you, that's just it,
Everything seems like the world's come to an end,
Your feelings in tatters, your heart won't mend,
People say kind words and pat your hand,
You feel like screaming, "YOU JUST DON'T UNDERSTAND!"
Everyone needs to work it out their own way,
You'll find me there, all you need to do is pray,
I don't just mean by clasping your hands,
I mean from the heart because spirit understands,
When you show that you're ready to be given the help you need,
Trust in yourself, and spirit and they'll plant that tiny seed,
The seed of faith, to yourself be true,
If you make mistakes, so what, we all do,
The cycle of life whether in spirit or earth plane,
Gives us the chance to get it right again.

A smile means a lot, so I wrote this poem to illustrate that. I have often caught a stranger's eye and smiled at them. Sometimes we've got talking and I've heard their life story. There are a lot of lonely people in the world and when you smile you give out positive vibes which draw people to you. My youngest son has learnt this art and makes friends wherever he goes, with people of all ages.

A SMILE

A smile costs nothing, it's for free,
An exchange of happiness between you and me,
It's worth far more than material riches,
It's simple to give and sent with fond wishes,
I know I can rely on a smile back from you,
You lift my spirits and stop me feeling blue,
We don't even have to speak in the same tongue,
It's something that should be for everyone,
A true friend is someone to cherish and love,
Priceless, and heaven sent, a gift from above.

There have been a few times in life when I've wondered how on earth I am going to climb out of the pit I seemed to find myself in. Then something has happened to turn it around completely in the most unlikely way. For example, when I split up with a partner I lived with for two years I was left with nowhere to live, no job, because I had worked for him and no car, because it belonged to his company. Most of my personal belongings were left behind and I didn't really have a lot going for me. Fortunately my sister let me stay with her for 6 weeks until I found myself somewhere to live for me and two children. The house I found to rent had white goods so that was a good start. I brought a few other small things from jumble sales and car boots but I had hardly any furniture. On the day I moved in I found the house was partly furnished with brand new double beds and a leather 3 piece suite, dining table etc. My ex partner seemed to come to his senses and return my belongings, it all fell into place. I couldn't believe my luck, or was it just luck? I've come to the conclusion that I must have a very good guardian angel, so that's where 'Put your trust in me' comes from.

Put Your Trust in Me

I'm in the sky and in the earth,
I'm in despair and I'm in mirth,
I'm in all of you, yes everyone,
I'm in the moon and in the sun.

If only you would put your trust in me,
That's the answer, that's the key,
The way to make your spirit free.

You ask the question, why are we here?
Just trust in me and you'll lose your fear,
If you trust in spirit, you will find,
You'll not have such a burdened mind.

If only you would put your trust in me,
That's the answer, that's the key,
The way to make your spirit free.

That you cannot see me, do not care,
For I am around you everywhere,
When the whole world's closing in and you want to run,
I am the answer, I'm the one.

I wrote 'Enjoy the present moment' because you often hear people beating themselves up over their past, and I have been guilty of this. The past is gone and all we can do is learn from it or remember happy times and be glad we experienced them. The future is uncertain so what's the point of worrying about it. All we can be sure of is the present, so make the most of it.

ENJOY THE PRESENT MOMENT

Life has problems for us to bear,
Sometimes it's hard to find an answer there,
We all need courage to face our day,
Just keep looking forward and you'll find a way.

Don't look back and don't look down,
Don't greet the world with a troubled frown,
Just enjoy the present moment for that's where the power lies,
The circle of life means that our spirit never dies.

It's just the outer packaging that falls into decay,
Out spirit keeps evolving, growing stronger every day,
Look within yourself and the answers you will find,
Ask for guidance to ease your troubled mind.

Live for the moment and life will flow more free,
We all need to simply be.

I wrote 'Driving Force' because throughout your life you will always be learning, you will never know it all. So we are all learners, and if we remember that it helps to be a little more tolerant towards others and not so hard on yourself.

Driving Force

Throughout our life we're always learning to find our way,
Nobody's perfect and won't be come what may,
If we had all the answers we really wouldn't be here,
So try to help each other and it will become more clear,

We've all got faults and made mistakes,
I think that we should wear L plates.

Life can take many twists and turns,
So just steer your course and try to learn,
For what you give out will surely come back,
So try to drive straight and keep on the right track,

We've all got faults and made mistakes,
I think that we should wear L plates.

Sometimes life feels like a hill start,
Just cover your brakes, don't try to be smart,
Sometimes we need to step back, to find out what to do,
Like reversing round a corner, you need a good view,

We've all got faults and made mistakes,
I think we all should wear L plates.

Use all your mirrors and look all around,
Consider other people and your judgement will be sound,
Don't go too fast and don't go too slow,
When you get up to the Test Centre you will really know,

We've all got faults and made mistakes,
I think we all should wear L plates,

Did we pass first time or have a few tries,
Can we throw away our L plates and hold our head up high,
Or will we have to come back and re-train,
I hope I don't have to take my test again.

I wrote 'Moving on Up' because I feel that when we pass over to spirit then this is what happens. It's only the physical body that is gone, not the spirit.

Moving on Up

Do not be afraid for I will be by your side,
I'll lead you, I'll be your light and guide,
Together we'll walk towards the light,
Have courage there is no need to fight,
For your time has come to move on up,
To higher levels and to take the golden cup,
The cup that brims over with great love,
We've learnt our lessons now we go above,
It's like we go into another room,
There is no darkness, it's like a sweep with a new broom,
The room is near and yet unseen,
Our friends and loved ones as if behind a silver screen,
Our pains and ills will go like they were never there,
We will emerge like we have climbed the stairs,
Or sometimes it's like rushing down a tunnel of light,
We come out the other side with new found sight,
Our lives are shown, right and wrong to compare,
So our soul learns what it needed to bear,
For when we return to earth's turbulent plane,
Unfinished issues will be there to retrain,
So that our soul is able to one day,
Guide others on their Spiritual Pathway.

I wrote 'More than I can say' for my dear friend June who I have know for sixteen years. She used to live two doors down the street from me and we have helped each other through many a dilemma. How lucky to have good friends!

More Than I Can Say

We share a special friendship, and both have similar views,
We've known each other many years, and been in many stews,
I know we are not friends by chance, it was arranged by those on high,
I'm glad that they ordained it, and I know the reason why.

For more than words can tell you, more than I can say,
You've been there in dark hours and brought light to my day.

We've both been sorely tested, we've both had to be strong,
Sometimes it's been so tempting to take revenge against the wrongs,
We both know that's not the answer, two wrongs don't make a right,
We've had to turn the other cheek and follow our spiritual light.

For more than words can tell you, more than I can say,
You've been there in dark hours, and brought light to my day.

Nothing could replace you, you're someone I can trust,
We've also shared the good times and laughed until we bust,
But if we didn't know bad times, we wouldn't appreciate good, would we?
For in life there's a need for balance, I know that's how it should be.

For more than words can tell you, more than I can say,
You've been there in dark hours and brought light to my day.

When I wrote 'What am I' I was looking back on my life and although I have had times of having not a lot in the material sense, as in struggling financially, I have always had some really great friends and family around me for love and support. To me that is more important than anything else. There is nothing worse than feeling alone!

WHAT AM I?

I can be given and I can be received,
You can feel me but you cannot see me,
I can sometimes cause pain, but everybody needs me,
whether they are young, old,
man, woman or child.
You can shun me or welcome me with open arms,
I cannot be measured in any way, shape or form,
Everybody can possess me if they choose to open their heart to me,
I can make you feel better in the twinkling of an eye,
I'm all around you, all you have to do is reach out and I'm there,
You cannot buy me although there are some that think you can,
You won't see me in a packet on a supermarket shelf,
WHAT AM I THEN?
I AM LOVE!

I wrote 'Moving On' as a way of voicing how I felt about getting divorced. I know that in general society thinks that divorce is too easy, but I also think that you need both people to be fully committed to making a marriage work and if one isn't then it becomes a hard battle. However, from my point of view I don't think there is any point in being bitter about it, we were married for ten years and had three sons. We have both moved on, he has re-married and I live with my partner and I am happy.

Moving On

I walked away from you it's true, but my reason was quite sound,
You didn't love me as I needed, you just messed me around,
I thought you'd understand one day and maybe you would change,
But I was wrong to think that way, some things are unexplained,
We started off so much in love but soon that feeling went,
I began to realise that I was not content,
You shouted and you bullied and left me alone to cope,
So I figured I would leave you and there would be more hope,
I wished that we could still be friends for our children's sake,
But to stay together for them would have been a big mistake,
Many years have passed now and my love for you long gone,
But I don't bear you any malice and we have both moved on.

We all have moments, at any stage in life where we feel that it's not fair. I remember one of my sons liked this phrase when he was about fourteen. There have been fleeting moments when I've been an adult that I could have agreed.

It's Not Fair

Feeling sorry for myself,
There's people worse, but that doesn't help,
Do I have to come back to this earth plane,
I don't want to see the sorrow and pain,
I've tried to be nice, Is it too much to ask,
That people are nice back, is it such a hard task?

All I know is IT'S NOT FAIR,
I need to find an answer there.

Have you got no money, trouble with the other half,
No hot water when you want to have a bath,
Have your children played you up, has your job application failed,
Are you wanting to get somewhere but the train's de-railed,
Has your washing machine broken, has your car given up,
What shall we blame it on, just bad luck?

All I know is IT'S NOT FAIR,
I need to find an answer there.

Does it seem that whatever you do you never get things right,
Do you sit and puzzle and try with all your might,
Can you sort everybody's problems, but struggle with your own,
Do you ever really think that you must be all alone,
Do you put your washing on the line and it suddenly pours with rain,
Do you start another diet and find it's all in vain,

All I know is IT'S NOT FAIR,
I need to find an answer there.

Sitting thinking rationally now, I'm told it's a learning curve,
Well I think I've learnt enough now, I think you've got a nerve,
But I know that in reality it's the only way to grow,
If we knew it all when we started out there would be no where to go,
We all need to take the rough with the smooth,
We all need to slot in the right groove,

So all I know now is that IT IS FAIR,
I think I've just found the answer there.

I decided to write 'Sorry I'm Late' when I worked in community care. We were often given an unrealistic time span in which to complete our calls and sometimes people understandably became a little put out. It was beyond our control so you just had to do your best. However, I think that some of the clients could have thought we just made it all up.

Sorry I'm Late

Sorry I'm late the carer said,
As she nervously stood at the end of my bed,
I wonder what the excuse would be today,
I pinned back my ears whilst she explained the delay,
But my eyes glazed over, someone had gone sick,
And that she'd had to cover, we all know that old trick,
It's almost as good as 'the cheques in the post'
Do they think I'm stupid, well I'm smarter than most,
Parts of my body may have gone into decline,
But please don't mistake that I'm losing my mind,
I know that you're busy, I know that you care,
But please don't just give me that wide innocent stare,
I've heard all the excuses, they go something like this,
It's the office's fault, oh please give it a miss,
You were stuck in a traffic jam, you couldn't get through,
Or you couldn't leave someone all covered in pooh,
Your cars had a flat tyre, or just broken down,
The police closed the roads on your side of the town,
I'll tell you what the truth is most likely to be,
You pulled into a lay-by and just sat drinking tea,
You probably read the newspaper or looked at a magazine,
Or maybe filed your nails or sat and day dreamed,
Or you listened to the radio and sang along to your favourite song,
Don't mind me love, I've got all day long,
So pick up the phone and explain and then I won't stress,
I know that all I ask of you the answer's usually yes,
So I promise then I'll understand, I won't get in a state,
The next time that you say to me 'SORRY I'M LATE'.

I wrote 'Rainbow of Life' because colour plays such an important part in our lives. Research has found that the colours that surround us, in our homes and places of work, and even in the clothes that we wear can have an affect upon us.

Rainbow of Life

We come into the world naïve and untainted,
But life's a rainbow of colours just waiting to be painted,
When we are young you could say we are green,
We know nothing of life, that is yet unseen,
At school we sometimes fear that we'll be called yellow belly,
It's hard to rebel against the pack, when your stomach feels like jelly,
When we become teenager's we sometimes may feel blue,
Trying to find where we fit in is often hard to do,
When we get married our partners may make us see red,
But it's just learning to compromise is what stands us in good stead,
When you are feeling ill, you may look white as a sheet,
Hopefully we regain our sparkle and get back on our feet,
If you don't want to end up orange, go easy with fake tan,
You'll look just like a footballer's wife but you won't have too many fans,
Sometimes when things go wrong our future may look black,
Having trust in something will get us back on track,
We say we're feeling in the pink and everything is rosy,
Love is all around us and everything's just so cosy,
Many people spend life searching for that ultimate pot of gold,
You won't find it at the rainbows end, it's for you to unfold.

This poem about my Grandad is about the happy memories that I have of him. He was diagnosed with Parkinsons Disease when he was in his seventies and when my Nan passed away when I was thirteen he came to live with us for two years. He had lots of stories that he liked to tell and I remember being fascinated by them.

Grandad

I remember fondly when I sat upon your knee,
All the amazing stories you would tell to me,
Sometimes about things that you had done when you were a boy,
Some were about the people whose company you'd enjoyed,
Some were silly stories, the truth I couldn't define,
About men who worked in cheese quarries and down the treacle mines,
You once worked with horses and were a keeper of the hounds,
But once you met your sweetheart your love it knew no bounds,
You worked hard and raised four children through happy times and sad,
You called these times the good old days, to look back made you glad,
You tried to get me to solve riddles and build towers of playing cards,
Your favourite trick was to watch carefully and then stamp your feet so hard,
I knew what you were up to but I just played along,
You also enjoyed singing and knew all the old time songs,
You loved to work in your garden and grew fruit, vegetables and flowers,
I would often find you there and spend many happy hours,
An illness took your body over and your hands began to shake,
The treatment that was available not much difference did it make,
When Nan died you came to live with us, the days must have seemed so long,
Just looking out of the window, your light then rarely shone,
But all that I can say to you is you really were the best,
I know you went to be with Nan and now you are at rest.

This very short poem 'Not Good Enough' sums up something that someone said to me one day which made me think. People waste so much time worrying about whether they are good enough. All you have to do is be yourself.

NOT GOOD ENOUGH

Not good enough,
Not good enough for who,
All you have to remember,
Is that you're good enough for you.

The number of times I have listened to stories where people in relationships pull each other to pieces are unfortunately many. I don't understand why you would do this to someone that you are supposed to love. However I have seen it from both sides where men try to humiliate their wives and where wives belittle their husbands. It's just a pointless power struggle.

If You Ever Leave Me

You'll never manage without me,
You're weak, you're useless, just you see,
You can't even operate the lawn mower,
Nobody likes you, there's nobody lower,
You can't drive the car on a motorway,
And your looks are all frumpy you've had your day,
I can do the shopping much more cheaply than you,
You don't do any work all day, you haven't a clue,
Your parents tell you what to do, you're right under their thumb,
But you just listen to them because you are so dumb,
If you ever leave me I never will forgive,
I'll make your life so difficult you just won't want to live,
You know I'm telling perfect truth, you don't like to hear,
So just make sure you listen to me and there's nothing for you to fear.
Oh I'll manage without you alright, it's taken me years to understand,
You're just a control freak, who likes the upper hand,
My love for you has slowly died like a withering flower,
You are your own worst enemy, now you're losing power,
I have many friends to help me, It couldn't be worse on my own,
It really isn't possible to feel anymore alone,
Who are you going to blame now that my Dad has passed away,
I'm sure you'll think of something, it's another game for you to play,
But now your game is over, because now I'm feeling stronger,
If I listened anymore I'd have my sanity no longer,
I don't care now what you think of me, I may not always be right,
The only thing I know for sure is that I don't want the fight,
So I'll release us both from the prison and then we'll both be free,
You can be happy spending all day in the pub and I'll be happy to be me.

This poem is for all the people who have ever been on a long car journey with children. I don't need to say any more than that!

Are We There Yet?

Off on holiday, car packed fit to burst,
A long drive and three children, so I expected the worst,
Three boys in the back seat ready to moan and fret,
Loads of time to pick fights and ask are we there yet?
We left our house only ten minutes ago,
I answer them sweetly "the time will soon go"

Why don't we play a game, what about I Spy,
OK then they agree, the minutes will fly,
After about fifteen minutes the youngest one moans,
They're making it too hard Mum and they won't leave me alone,
And it's not very long before I break out in a sweat,
As they utter the question "Are we there yet?"

They're pushing and shoving, I tell them to stop,
Would they prefer walking but I don't blow my top,
I just count to ten and think up something else to play,
But very soon it ends in much the same way,
For a while two decide to have a little snooze,
The other one keeps quiet and we just seem to cruise,

An hour passes and I hear an anguished cry,
Mum I need the loo, so I look for a lay-by,
Then they decide they want something to eat,
So I get out their lunchboxes and find them a treat,
We get back in the car and off we all set,
When I'm plagued by the sound of "Are we there yet?"

As we climb a steep hill the car complains at the load,
I try to keep my eyes fixed firmly on the road,
We come to a halt at some traffic lights,
I've eaten too much because my seat belt is too tight,
I look at my watch well we're over half way,
Hopefully we will arrive around midday,

It seems now it's question time and I'm in the mastermind seat,
I've ten minutes on everything there is to know and I don't want to be beat,
After they've exhausted every subject and seem satisfied,
I thank heaven my prayers have been answered and we've finally arrived,
But it seems there's one winning question, how could I forget,
The three of them chorus "ARE WE THERE YET!"

My youngest son always encourages me to step out of my comfort zone and try something new. He has brought new clients to me by chatting to people about the job I do which is a Holistic Therapist. He also encourages me with the poetry writing and jokingly said to write a poem about him. So that's what I did.

My son

My son asked me to write this poem,
So that you reader will come to know him,
He's smart, he's clever, he's a star,
I've always known that he'll go far,
He's always ready to lend a hand,
He's always willing to understand,
He enjoys his sports, he works hard at school,
He only sometimes acts the fool,
He likes kick boxing, he enjoys scouts,
On his bike he's out and about,
He always likes to be on the go,
He's just a human dynamo,
Why did I write this, you may ask,
He whittled me and set me the task,
He is my helper, he's my chum,
I should know because I am his Mum,
I hope this rhyme is ok son,
Because you're not getting another one.

I wrote this poem about money as I have seen people with hardly any who seem quite content with life and I have seen people with an excess who are miserable. People strive for it, thinking it will make them happier. I think that is more likely to be the case if you are happy in the first place.

Money

It's trouble when you haven't got it and trouble when you do,
It's what makes the world go round, it can really make you blue,
To work we go and earn it, doing work that we don't care for,
It goes into our bank account but we always seem to need more,
I wish that all the bills would go to the wrong address,
I'll strike a bargain with the postman and that will be less stress,
I know that won't work really, but I can dream can't I,
Maybe I'll win the lottery, then I'll be on a high.

I have two older sisters so I felt my job was to be a first class pest. One of them is eight years older than me so had to look after me sometimes.

SISTER

Sister, dear Sister I know I'm a pain,
You've been there for me time and time again,
When I was born you brought friends to see me sleeping sound,
That peace didn't last, you knew that I was around,
When we were children you had me tagging along,
You really had your work cut out showing me right from wrong,
You never married and had children, so were second Mum to mine,
It was good to borrow them and give them back was your favourite line,
How lucky I am to have someone like you,
Someone to rely on, someone who is true.

I often hear people complain that they have been let down by someone. I feel it is a mistake to rely on someone else to make you happy. To share your life with someone is a good thing, but to rely on them for everything is quite different. I've found that to be responsible for yourself works much better.

EMPTY PROMISES

People often ask me why I don't ask them to assist,
It would take a long time to explain, but now I can't resist,
I've had so many empty promises that have not been kept,
Ones that I built my hopes upon and in the past I have wept,
I'm not talking of little promises but of ones promising to commit,
So now I only trust a few, I'm not going to submit,
The promises they come gushing to win your favours fair,
But then they get you where they want you and then they declare,
That they don't know what I'm talking about,
It's in my imagination, they never said nowt,
Well my imagination must certainly be vivid,
I don't sit and analyse it or I would just become livid,
So now I just take life as it comes and rely on me alone,
I'll share my time with others but the answers are my own.

Sometimes we have to use 'tough love' with our offspring. What works with one child does not work with another As our children become older we cannot bail them out of everything. It isn't as simple as when they were younger and they cut their knee and you picked them up, comforted them and made it better. The older they become the more outside influences and peer pressure come into play. It can be hard to watch them make the mistakes, but sometimes the more you tell them not to do something the more they rebel. The hard bit is watching them suffer the consequences of their actions. Usually they come through the other side but you will always love your children.

LOVE ALWAYS

I know we've had our differences, to say otherwise wouldn't be true,
I've tried so hard to do the right things, but I am human too,
I've had to watch you struggle with life and go through a lot of pain,
I've shed more tears than could fill the ocean but life's turned around again,
When we raise our children, they don't come with individual instructions,
Of how to handle or operate, so no surprise there can be ructions,
You can read all the experts books but they can't predict every situation,
It's something you learn as you go along, it's one big education,
I remember the day you were born and I thought what have I done?
The feeling of responsibility enormous, but I've always loved you son,
Although there have been tough times and some very long nights and days,
A love of a mother for her children is simply LOVE ALWAYS.

I always wonder why we get fooled into paying out lots of money for things like clothes and handbags. I realize the fashion industry has to make a living but most things are really over priced. The fashion designers must be laughing all the way to the bank.

Follower of Fashion

Do you buy clothes just because they are the fashion,
Does your rationale get overtaken by your passion,
Do you buy into the latest healthy eating craze,
Or follow bizarre diets and feel like you're in a half starved daze,
Do you walk lopsided because of that heavy designer bag on your shoulder,
Really you should stop and think, be a little bolder,
All these things that you must have will cost you lots of money,
Just develop your own style and that's just sweet as honey.

Lots of people these days love the many antiques and collectables programmes that are shown on television. I must admit I do enjoy going round car boot sales and charity shops. When I was a child I would go with my Mum and my Sister to the local jumble sales and my Mum would be first in the queue. When the doors were opened she would have her elbows out and head straight for the bric brac stall. No one was going to get past her. She would buy her bargains and take them home where my Dad would shake his head and laugh at her. What she did then was to take them to a local antique shop where she had struck up a rapport with the owner and sell them for a profit.

BARGAIN HUNT

Scan the car boot sale and charity shop,
I must find that bargain, I can't resist, I can't stop,
I've watched Car Booty, Flog It and Antiques Roadshow,
I'm in seach of a rarity, when I see it I'll know so,
China, or furniture, clocks or fine art,
I'm sure I'll find my prize it's so dear to my heart,
I know that it's out there somewhere and when I find it you will see,
I'm dreaming of retiring because I'll make loads of money,
But for now I'll keep on searching it gives me such a kick,
It's a great big battle, just watch the dealers up to tricks,
It's quite something to watch the pushing and grunting,
I know that I've just got to keep on hunting.

I had to re-home my dogs when my personal circumstances changed and I could no longer keep them. The people who they went to had just retired so could spend lots of time with them. It was a hard thing to do but the kindest.

Faithful Friend

You always barked when people come to the door,
You always came to greet me, your paws pattering on the floor,
You would escape from the garden and chase after cats,
It didn't matter if I called you because you just felt like a spat,
You liked playing a game, you were full of fun,
You'd find a patch in the garden and lay in the sun,
You liked burying things and chewing shoes,
You always got the other half's, never mine would you choose,
We'd lay on the sofa, your head next to mine,
We'd keep each other warm so that was just fine,
You would scavenge in bins to find bones and scraps,
You'd drive everyone crazy with your terrier yaps,
I'll never forget you, I'll love you always,
Unconditional love and no price to pay.

My Grandad always used to say that a drunk man's words were a sober man's mind and I definitely agree. It's just an excuse to say what you like. That's ok if you like living dangerously, but not my idea of fun.

A Drunk Man's Words

Enjoying a drink is one thing, but don't make it a full time career,
You're not very good to be around if you're constantly reeking of beer,
In your company it can be precarious to know just how to be,
If we keep quiet we're in a mood with you,
if you speak your words are twisted you see,
It's a no win situation and you'll swear blind never, no more,
But we've all heard that one many, many times before,
A drunk man's thoughts is a sober man's mind,
If your tongue gets looser when you drink, unlucky for you you'll find,
So just be careful what you say "I was just joking," say some!
But in my experience lies will bite you on the bum.

I really love spending time by the sea, it is so relaxing. I don't enjoy being locked indoors for any great length of time as I start to feel a bit caged up. How lucky we are to have large open spaces to be in, it cheers me up better than any shopping trip or night to the pub. If there is one thing I am, it is that I am cheap to run.

Spirit of the Sea

I love to listen to the sound of the sea,
Your mind can be calm and your thoughts more free,
Your troubles taken away by the retreat of the tide,
You can step off that daily roller coaster ride,
The sound of children's laughter carries on the breeze,
They've heard your call for help now, so get up off your knees,
The sound of seagulls punctuates your thinking,
Being in this space is stopping you from sinking,
We all need to collect our thoughts together,
Our mind can become too clouded, akin to stormy weather,
So take time away to simply be,
Connect with your surroundings and your mind will be free.

If you have ever looked at advertisements for cars the words they use can mean something entirely different. They have a language all of their own so I wrote this poem comparing a car to myself.

If I Were A Car

If I were a car what would I be,
I know I'd be a shiny red Lamborgini,
I'm swift on my feet so I'm like a fast car,
I'm really quite streamlined and I'd like to go far,
But that's just in my dreams so I better get real,
A second hand old motor is more like the deal,
My headlights are dim now and there's problems with my suspension,
My bodyworks starting to decline and definitely needs attention,
I've had one or two careless owners rather than one careful one,
I've raced around and I've rallied and I like to have fun,
But I suppose that there is one thing of which there is no fear,
In my advert you could say that I'm ok for my year.

Printed in the United Kingdom
by Lightning Source UK Ltd.
130019UK00001B/394/P